Numbers Scare Me & Other Excuses

A Business Owner's Guide to Lead Like a CFO

Josh Greenbaum

Praise for **Numbers Scare Me**

"Reading your book was ultimately the catalyst to getting our financials up to date — and I mean the *whole* deal: balance sheet, cash flow, P&L, operating expenses, break-even analysis. Even more than how the specific information was helpful, the setup of *why* this is so important sold me." —*Lee Maier, Co-Founder, Ted Time Co.*

"As a business owner, I always found the finances to be the most intimidating part of running my company. Josh was able to break things down and help me understand the financial aspect of my business in a way that made me feel knowledgeable and empowered. He taught me not only how to read and analyze financial statements, but also how to use them in my decision-making and goal-setting." —*Katie Wagner, President, KWSM: a digital marketing agency*

"Josh is a trustworthy and straightforward professional equipped with the relevant business advice needed for me to achieve the highest level of success. Throughout our journey together launching my startup, I've learned the power of numbers from the perspective of both a business operator and a

strategist. I have been empowered throughout the process to raise money and build my business, and am certain that no question is unanswerable."
— *Sarah Kraft, Founder & CEO, CheersMate*

"As my professional organizing business grew rapidly over its first few years, Josh helped organize us financially, setting up our bookkeeping systems and coaching us on how to manage them on a day-to-day basis, as well as guiding us through the transition from having independent contractors to employees. I feel so much more confident interpreting my company's numbers based on what I've learned from Josh and his book!"
— *Shara Kay, Certified Professional Organizer & Founder, SK Organizing*

"Josh is unlike any other CFO I've worked with. The process laid out in this book reinforced the importance of sticking to the margins I have set for my company and not wavering, which is what Josh taught me from day one. This has made all the difference and allows me to invest and expand the company in ways I never imagined."
— *Emma Greenbaum, Founder & CEO, Thriving Learners (No relation, just a wonderful coincidence)*

"As a small business owner, I appreciate having Josh as our numbers guy. He is more than a CFO — he has become a mentor and motivator to help take our business to the next level. The lessons in this book taught me to think big while making smart financial decisions and, most importantly, without losing the fun!" — *Katie Wafer, Founder & CEO, Hydrate IV Bar*

"Josh stepped in just prior to our staple event at the Super Bowl and implemented systems that allowed us to operate seamlessly and effectively. From that point forward, we've maintained these processes, which has enabled up to scale the volume of events, settle with partners quickly, and achieve greater profitability." — *Adam Richman & Joe Silberzweig, Founders, Medium Rare*

Dedicated to our small business owners
who give their energy and soul to our communities
and make the world thrive.

CONTENTS

INTRODUCTION

It pains me when I meet so many small business owners who are unclear of their company's financial position. They are left in the dark by bookkeepers who give them little more insight into their numbers than the balance of their online checking account. How is this okay? Some owners excuse this by saying they don't like accounting, but that doesn't mean they can ignore it. They've invested an unbelievable amount of time, tears, and money to launch and grow their business, only to be left with sleepless nights and no clear line of sight to the dollars and cents of the whole thing.

No more excuses.

It's easy for me to walk into your business, click through the QuickBooks file, and quickly assess problems and areas for improvement. That's what a great CFO does, but most business owners have no idea what to look for. Still, I want you to be able to easily assess your finances just like I would — and I believe you can learn how.

By virtue of you picking up this book, I feel invested in the success of your business and want to see you achieve everything you've dreamed because business is personal to me.

So my promise to you is that by the end of this book, you will have the confidence, framework, and increased financial literacy to effectively manage your team, take control of your money, and lead like a CFO!

———

My first job in college was at a local deli in San Luis Obispo, a sleepy town on California's central coast. Every morning, I'd wake up at 4 a.m. to bake fresh bread. We would mix batches of dough from scratch, weighing upward of 120 pounds, and roll it out on the weathered butcher block table.

Once the bread came out of the oven, I'd tend to the sandwich line and serve people from the community coming in for lunch, all while learning the ins and outs of a food-service small business. Even today, I look back at this as one of my favorite jobs because of the spirited folks with whom I worked, the personal interaction with our customers, and that feeling of accomplishment each day as fresh bread came out of the oven.

Eventually, the owner decided to expand the business next door and serve pizza. Because I'd done such a good job at the deli, he gave me the opportunity to create new recipes and play with toppings. Not only that, he encouraged me to dream of what this new pizza business could one day become. Suddenly, I had the chance to innovate and get my feet wet as a sort of stakeholder in the restaurant. I *loved* it.

My boss must have been impressed by my interest and dedication because after a while, he started including me in conversations about costs and pricing, staffing, and other elements pertinent to our day-to-day operations. I was thrilled! Years later, I even toyed with the idea of buying the business after college.

Though I ultimately chose a different career path, my time at the restaurant taught me one important lesson: *I loved small business.* I thrived being part of a lean and nimble team that could quickly create and execute to move an idea forward.

And numbers were always my thing. In fact, aside from running, math was the area of high school I excelled at the most, and a direction I saw myself going as a possible college major and career path. Though I was never the academic type, the part-time jobs I had in school really gave me enjoyment and perspective as I went through my business and accounting classes.

So it may be somewhat surprising that after graduating college, my first job was in Silicon Valley where I worked for one of the largest public accounting firms in the world, PricewaterhouseCoopers (PwC). I felt drawn to the firm because of the wonderful people I met there, as well as for the opportunity to be exposed to so many different types of businesses. And at that point, I knew that accounting was my strength, and serving others (customers/clients) made me happy, so the firm was a perfect place to launch my career.

As an Associate with PwC in its audit practice, I, along with my team, would typically come into public and private companies on behalf of a Board of Directors as an independent set of eyes on financial statements so that investors and other outside parties felt confident about the quarterly and annual information they received from internal management. This showed me how accounting departments were organized and the interrelation between each person.

I quickly learned about best practices, business processes, and business models for a variety of companies within the technology industry. It was great exposure to see the inner workings of venture capital, semiconductors, social media, software, and biotech! I had expected there to be big differences between the various types of businesses, so I was fascinated to learn how much they had in common.

While this massive corporate environment was the polar opposite of a small business, the work I did there built a strong working foundation of corporate accounting that taught me how to analyze and scale a business like a pro. Plus, I loved the client service aspect of my job and the variety it offered my day-to-day work. I encountered a wide range of professionals, businesses, and management styles and discovered I had a knack for attending to my clients personally.

After a couple of years, I transferred to our Los Angeles office and shifted my focus from tech to entertainment clients and spent much of my time on the DreamWorks Animation and Sony studio lots. While working with high-profile companies was exciting and I learned a ton, my time at such a large firm ultimately made me realize that what I really wanted was to return to small business.

I was reminded how much I liked being able to wrap my arms around a small business's whole operation and interact directly with the founder and the executive team. Though the accounting was sometimes simplistic, it reminded me how foundational it is for any size business, and how integral it is for growth and profit. I also began to do some financial modeling, which opened a creative side of my mind that I had not yet tapped into professionally. Finding this combination of accounting and financial modeling stirred in me a passion I hadn't previously recognized.

Did I lose you at "financial modeling"? In simple terms, it is a process that takes all the specific elements of the business plan and aligns them with the strategic plan to build, launch, or grow a company. It's like putting a puzzle together.

The first model I built was with a well-known celebrity in the music industry who was starting his first tech company. He needed me to build a model that would financially validate his assumptions, project those into the future, and ultimately help him raise money for his business from investors.

It's fair to say I was obsessed, working endlessly into the night (which was also a pretty good indicator that I should pay attention to and figure out how I could do this type of work more often). And in the end, I was able to be a part of the team who helped him raise enough capital to launch on a huge scale. He was happy, and a fire inside of me was ignited.

From that experience, I learned that even the most brilliant entrepreneurs and creative minds benefit from a financial professional who can take their big vision and translate it into a step-by-step plan. I also learned that I could shape my degree in accounting any way I wanted as I began to combine my education and my professional passions.

Feeling inspired, I took a leap from my regular job and what I knew was a traditionally stable career path, and began consulting. The uncertainty should have scared me more than it did, but this felt like a unique moment in time and, quite frankly, the old path bored me to death, so it wasn't really even a question. I met interesting people all the time who were making money through restaurants, bars, and music, and I wanted to work hand-in-hand with them.

So I grabbed control of my career, figured out QuickBooks on the fly, and asked a ton of questions to learn all the things I didn't know that I didn't know. Overall, these were the new tactical and operational skills that working in a large firm environment never taught me.

Soon, I was working with truly incredible people — music managers; world-renowned DJs and artists; a TV executive; tech founders; music festival operators; retail shop owners and franchisors; restaurateurs; social media marketers; educational service providers; a C-suite executive search firm . . . Definitely *not* boring.

I felt truly honored to work with these clients because each one taught me something new. And, because I take my client relationships seriously and personally, every one of them felt like family to me.

The lesson I took away is that large corporations are simply complex small businesses. The principles and practices are just as necessary to you as a small business owner as they are to the big guys. For this reason, I want you to understand the fundamentals even if you don't have the financial means to build an entire accounting and finance team.

Now, lest you think I made this leap and everything worked out easily and perfectly, here's a reality check: my income dropped substantially. So, while this time was exciting, it was also emotionally and financially tough. One day, though, I realized one of the most valuable lessons I learned on this journey was that . . .

I WAS AN ENTREPRENEUR!

I had been so immersed in my work as a service provider that it took me a while to realize I was also a business owner. Now I had to think a lot more about all those things I had been preaching. And believe me when I tell you that I made *all* the mistakes of many new consultants and entrepreneurs. I lived the ultimate cliché that it's easy to give advice but hard to take it yourself.

What would I tell a client to do in the same circumstance? I desperately needed to take my own advice, so I hired various coaches and embraced the chance for self-improvement. After all, the one constant in my business was me, so over the following year, I got very clear on questions I had avoided answering:

- Who did I want to be as a professional?
- Who was my target client?
- What service(s) did I want to offer?
- What did I want for my business?

These are questions you too must ask yourself.

I embraced that I was a boutique service provider who gave personal attention to my clients, and *that* was a premium service. I started to flesh out my SMART (Specific, Measurable, Achievable, Relevant, Time-based) goals because I knew what I needed most was a life design. Until I could define what I wanted in my life and what I valued, everything would continue in a meaningless direction.

—

This is when I really learned how essential non-financial goals were for business owners.

So I outlined my new rates alongside the services I really wanted to provide — the work I did best. I defined specifically who I was as a professional and who I wanted to be for my clients. Along with a rebrand and a new website, I updated my own accounting so I could measure how everything progressed.

Moving forward, I set minimum retainers for new clients so I could target the amount of money I wanted to earn in the year ahead without overextending myself. This set me on a path for financial success.

I then made an investment in my own business and took out a small business loan so I could grow, which allowed me to comfortably hire an accounting manager who assisted with client work and oversaw an outsourced bookkeeping firm. With this infrastructure, I could continue building my client base and achieve the lifestyle I desired.

My core values emerged as **consistency, transparency, and open communication** because small business owners wear many hats, and time is precious. What they need most are numbers delivered in a timely fashion, usable and functional financial information, and an open line to them as an integral part of the management team. It was off of these pillars that I built my **Process • Plan • Path** framework, which allows me to be transparent in the CFO role. We'll dig into the framework more throughout this book, but in short, it's a cycle of brainstorming and strategic goal setting, establishing a financial plan, taking action, and producing standard accounting deliverables. I implement this framework in every client's business to not only enhance their accounting processes, but also to help them identify and build a solid plan to achieve their goals, big and small.

The purpose of this book is to bring financial sophistication to every business — to get past the set-it-and-forget-it mentality of accounting, eliminate financial question marks, and get clearer on how to reach your most aspirational goals.

Which leads me to you. The business owner or aspiring entrepreneurs who picked up this book.

Like my clients, you feel like family to me. You invested in me by reading this book, so I'm invested in the success of your business and want to see you achieve everything you've dreamed because business is personal to me.

I'm going to take a few guesses about who you are and how you might feel right now about your business's finances. I have a hunch you've thought — and maybe said — at least a few of the following things about your money and your business:

"I'm so scared of numbers! They freak me out!"

"I feel disconnected from what my accountant is doing."

"I have no clue what's going with my finances. Are my books being done correctly?"

"I'm exhausted and burned out!"

"I know what my financial goals are, but I have no idea how to reach them."

"I don't know how to reach the next financial level in my business."

This probably sounds familiar to you, right? Well, you're not alone.

Even the wildly successful clients I've worked with, at one point or another, share these thoughts with me. I have always implicitly interpreted this as their desire for more transparency with their accounting. And while open communication is obviously essential in that relationship, as the business owner, it's up to you to set the standard for how people who work for you report to you.

Don't play victim to a circumstance you created through a lack of financial literacy. I believe you can learn the basics of accounting and finance and take control. Define how your accountant will report to you, and if they don't deliver, get a new accountant.

Through my work with various clients at different stages of their business's growth, I realized that so much came down to their mindset. Like me in the early stages of my entrepreneurial journey, they may not yet have the confidence and skill set of a seasoned CEO and are often intimidated by finance. I often witness their imposter syndrome or limiting beliefs around what it means to be the boss.

There's a whole new level of expertise and responsibility that comes along with running a business. First and foremost is to command the revenue needed to support yourself and your business through good times and bad. Often new business owners, and specifically solo entrepreneurs, end up making the same amount of money they did in corporate life for the tradeoff of freedom. Freedom is great and all, but so was that steady paycheck you had — something not guaranteed when working for yourself.

Pro Tip: If you made $100,000 in your job and you want to make $100,000 in your consulting business, aim for $200,000 in revenue. More on this concept later in the book when we discuss Gross Profit Margin.

Leaving your corporate job does *not* buy freedom: *financial success* buys freedom, and you have to aim for the right numbers to get there. Freedom to take on projects you love and turn down the clients whom you don't align with; freedom from the worry of next month's bills; freedom to create a business that you can sell.

Many business owners benefit from a strong CFO to mentor and encourage them, to challenge them, to play devil's advocate. To hear them out on the good, bad, and ugly, and remind them of their end goals. That's what a good advisor does, and that's who you want on your financial team.

And that's the role I play: a kind of business coach who helps my clients identify limiting beliefs and make paradigm shifts that free them to confidently and competently run their business like a true business. It's actually one of the things I love most about what I do.

Part of being a good coach is creating space and clarity for clients so they can define their goals and make the best decisions for themselves. So let me be very clear about who this book is for:

- Entrepreneurs with a clear business vision who are ready to take the leap.
- Business owners (solo service providers, this means you too!) who haven't yet reached their financial goals.
- Business owners who need to learn how to create systems and processes.
- Business owners who want to feel more confident in guiding their business where they want it to go.

- Business owners who may or may not yet be clear on their goals for their business and need guidance to identify them.
- Business owners who want to put more money in their pocket.

If this is you, I am thrilled you're here. You are my people. And here's what I envision you taking away from this book:

- Clarity about your business goals and the steps you need to take to reach them.
- Up-leveled understanding about and comfort with your finances.
- Increased confidence in your ability to take control of your business's finances and team.
- Knowledge and tools to create a solid strategy to help your business grow and to build a cohesive team all working toward the same goals.

The most important thing to know, especially if accounting or money has intimidated you up to this point, is that you have the power to flip the script.

You control the numbers; they don't control you.

Recognize that numbers tell the truth one hundred percent of the time. Many business owners tend to rely on their intuition or gut feelings around money and finances, but that may get you in trouble fast.

———

Truly successful business owners know their business and industry inside-out and see numbers as a useful tool to help validate and direct their decisions.

They have clearly articulated goals and a straightforward path to achieving them. Because of this, they know which roles and responsibilities are necessary within the organization to deliver on those goals. Every team member is clear about the part they play and the value it brings. Furthermore, the numbers may be an early indicator that it's time to enact change.

Clear thought leads to clear and effective communication, and this is what helps great businesses thrive.

Business owners who employ smart, thoughtful strategies also know how to identify and clear obstacles that threaten to derail them — including their own blind spots!

I was once told by a client that there are two types of CEOs: marketing (left brain) and financial (right brain). Most people naturally excel one way or another, and, by definition, are not as strong in the other areas. When a leader understands where they need help, they can balance out their executive team with people who complement their natural skills and bring different perspectives to the table.

Be honest with yourself about where you are strongest and where you need to shore up support to make yourself a better leader. That honesty about your business's finances will strengthen you because you can't build a healthy company on a foundation of wishful thinking and avoidance of the true numbers.

It doesn't have to be scary, though. One of the biggest things I want you to take away from this book is that you are more than capable of understanding your business's numbers and making sound financial decisions. You just need a system to guide you through the process.

And, fortunately for you, I've created one that clearly and simply lays out three essential concepts that you can easily integrate into your daily financial life, both professionally and personally.

This framework — Process • Plan • Path — helps you organize your financial activity in a systematic way, takes the fear out of working with your numbers, shows you how to establish appropriate goals for your stage in business, and gives you the steps to take to consistently reach them.

Ready? Let's do this!

PART 1

————

The Framework

1

ESTABLISH A FOUNDATION

After nearly 20 years working in the accounting industry, I discovered something all businesses have in common that led me to develop a core framework on which I base all my client consulting engagements. As I clarified the smartest approach for both my clients' businesses and my own business, I knew I needed to address three main components of a healthy and growing company:

1. **A succinct and specific business plan.**
2. **An executable financial roadmap and cash flow management.**
3. **Complete, accurate, and measurable results.**

I found that in every case, regardless of industry or business type, these three elements were foundational and essential for that business to thrive. They also required constant attention.

When I look at these elements through the lens of a CFO, I think: business (accounting) processes, business plan, and budgets. I refer to these simply as **Process • Plan • Path**, which we'll explore in more detail throughout the book.

Establishing systems helps your business run more smoothly, but accounting is not a set-and-forget-it kind of thing. The processes are ongoing and need attention, nurturing, and constant refinement to see what is and is not working.

I start at Process for a very specific reason: Whether you have an existing company or are in the early stages of starting a company, you must have a firm grasp of your financial situation in order to properly look toward the future. From there, the framework is a continuous cycle.

When you learn this cycle for your own business, you'll become a strong financial leader — CFO Minded.

2

PROCESS • PLAN • PATH

Surprise! Most companies don't actually have their act together when it comes to accounting. That's a big reason most companies barely make it.

So let's start with a quick overview of the three core elements, which I'll collectively refer to as the Accounting Cycle Framework. This chapter may have concepts with which you're not yet familiar, but don't worry, you'll get the hang of it. I've also included a glossary at the end for quick reference.

And I'll provide brief, real-life examples so you can get a better sense of how these concepts are applied in different kinds of businesses. Remember, the goal is for you to grasp this framework so you can better manage your team, fully understand your financial statements, and create processes that give you a simple but complete snapshot of your financial information every month.

My goal is not to turn you into an accountant because your time is better spent on other parts of your business. I simply want you to gain confidence in your financial leadership.

Process

First, you must dive into the nitty-gritty accounting stuff, including financial statements, management reports, key performance indicators (KPIs), and checklists, and focus on key processes that will keep your financial house running smoothly — and, most importantly, keep you informed!

You want to create high-quality accounting so you know you're getting the most accurate information from which to make decisions. You might think this is standard practice in business accounting, but unfortunately, it's really easy for accountants to take shortcuts that make their job easier and the deliverables they provide just "good enough." Put another way, they aim for just passing, while I want you to get an A+.

During the Process stage, the individual business transactions — invoicing a new client or selling a cup of coffee — turn into account balances, which are regularly reviewed. Then your accountant adjusts those numbers into accrual accounting (to be defined later) so they are meaningful. Finally, financial statements are prepared for you to evaluate and analyze.

You can think of this process as a regular check-up for the health of your company and the success of your business plan. In this stage, we pull everything together in a nice, organized package that ensures you consistently see results in your business, meet your goals, and can course-correct as needed.

The most important thing I can communicate to you in this entire book is to learn to whittle down your financial statements to a single-page summary, which I refer to as an *Executive Financial Dashboard*. To be an effective leader in your business, you need to have a holistic view of the financial state of your business.

Best practices in your accounting and financial systems, strong controls around cash management, and a timely system for reporting are all vital to the financial well-being of your company. If you receive financial information too long after the end of the month, you may miss opportunities to quickly pivot in response to unproductive practices or to stop unnecessary cash bleeds. Not being able to promptly address problems loses you time and money — neither of which you can spare in a small business.

For example, you may have software or services that you don't use and that cost you profit because they charge recurring fees. Alternatively, you may have a product that is mispriced and ultimately costs you money each time you sell one. If this is your hottest product, it could quickly sink your cash.

The systems I'll define and that you'll put in place will mitigate these risks. You will make it a practice to maintain a to-do checklist at the end of the month to ensure you haven't missed anything.

Once you make this a regular part of your work, your processes are reliable. This reliability also means you have set concrete expectations around these processes that you can communicate to internal and external teammates about how your accounting department must operate.

Now that these systems are in place, use your scheduled monthly check-ins to evaluate how everything is progressing so you can proactively:

1. Take the right actions to continue success and profitability, or
2. Pivot the timing and specifics of those goals, depending on what you learn.

In summary, the key action steps in the Process phase include:

- Creating a checklist of tasks that must be regularly completed.
- Closing the books monthly and having your accountant provide financial statements, inclusive of any relevant reports and KPIs, on a set deadline (e.g., by the 15th day of the following month).
- Keeping accounting records on an accrual basis.

—

- Establishing internal controls to reduce the chance of fraudulent transactions.

Plan

In addition to strong processes, every business owner must have a formal or informal business plan to be successful at any level. Putting one together usually involves brainstorming, research, a marketing plan, pricing strategy, and a SWOT (Strengths, Weaknesses, Opportunities, and Threats) analysis to hone those ideas.

I'm sure you have a good idea of what goes into a business plan, but this is often a step that small business owners skip in favor of jumping right into the work itself. Yet without a clear plan, the business may end up fragmented or unfocused and complicate the operations or introduce financial inefficiency. Also, many solo entrepreneurs don't think they need one because "it's just me" and plans to grow on a large scale either don't exist or aren't properly mapped out.

Some people can get by reasonably well without a clearly articulated plan. And some people make so much money that it's just easier to ignore the cash leaks. But at some point, they may hit a wall: the economy slows, their income sources dry up, the market shifts, they choose the wrong person for the wrong supporting role, or they run themselves ragged.

The truth is, you run a much higher risk of failing when you don't have a clear idea of who your best market is and how you fit in it; don't know the most effective way for your team members to function together; and don't have clarity on your processes and goals.

The same goes for accounting and finance. You must organize and operate in a way that translates the day-to-day data into useful information to manage your team (which might just be you).

In the Plan phase, I help my clients gain exacting clarity on high-level factors like:

- Financial parameters around the services or products they offer and how success is measured.
- A structured plan for the next six months, year, five years . . .
- Alignment of their personal goals as it relates to their business.
- Optimization of personal strengths within the organization.
- How to use their team's strengths (if they have a team) and identify gaps.

Other key objectives in formulating your Plan might include:

- Getting clear on your product/service mix and your pricing structure.
- Defining service deliverables, product logistics, and customer experience.

- Quantifying your marketing and customer acquisition plans.
- Creating a proper incentive compensation plan for your team (e.g., cash or equity).
- Calculating short-term cash flow to fund operations.

Path

Finally, the next logical step is to create a financial roadmap or path for you to reach the goals you've established.

I discovered that some of my clients were actually very clear on what they offered, how they made money, and what their goals were, but they had no idea how to estimate the investment capital needed to fund their growth, how to access capital from a bank, or even how to manage cash flow along the way. So they just grew more and more frustrated and felt buried in work.

For these types of clients, the first thing I do is map out a financial forecast by making assumptions about the future, assign the right people the right responsibilities, and plan for those unexpected twists and turns that inevitably arise. Furthermore, I define milestones and check-in points that indicate progress. In short, this process creates organization, structure, and intent. You'll then compare the forecast and the business plan side by side and make sure both tell the same story . . . which brings us back to Process, because the numbers in front of you are only as good as your accounting processes.

This is another place the work I do resembles business coaching more than accounting, which, as you'll recall, I totally love because business is personal.

The truth is, accounting is the lifeblood of your business. When it's a young startup, you must take extra care to nurture it, just like you would a newborn baby, except instead of regular bottles and diaper changes, you'll focus on cash flow for those times when revenue is low and expenses are high.

Then your business grows up a bit and begins to operate on its own as certain behaviors become second nature. And, just like children, as your business matures, it will continue to face new challenges, which we factor into your Plan and subsequent Path.

To summarize, the key elements in the Path stage include:

- Creating short-term goals for your business.
- Aligning a budget with milestones, anticipated sales, operational costs, and business goals.
- Using financial modeling to understand the bottom-line impact of various sales channels and scenarios.
- Documenting your assumptions and thought process as the budget is developed.
- Anticipating your capital needs.

- Planning your personnel growth through an organizational chart, which outlines team structure and the timing of hires.
- Communicating roles and responsibilities to your employees and contractors.

Now that you have the 30,000-foot view of the framework, I want to bring these ideas to life in more concrete and practical terms. So, moving forward, after I deep-dive into each phase, I'll give you examples of how three different businesses at different stages in their growth might implement those concepts, since each one has a distinct purpose and focus. I also hope you'll see your business in one (or more) of them and be able to determine your best path forward.

Meet the Businesses

Slow Drip Coffee is a new coffee shop that the owner, Erin, wants to open later this year, which is her primary goal when she comes to me. But, as she tells me, "I don't even know where to start!"

She has saved $25,000 to launch the business and has management background in retail and food operations, but no actual barista experience, nor has she run her own business before. However, she does know Jeff, who has been professionally involved in coffee distribution his whole life and recently won a local barista competition. Gotta love that latte art!

Dorothy Rose is a flower shop that its namesake, Dorothy, started fifteen years ago. She feels like life is passing her by and comes to me with the goal of spending less time in her business. Specifically, she wants to move from working six days a week to three days a week to enjoy more time traveling and being with family.

Dorothy Rose regularly earns $15,000 in gross revenue each month, and the business experiences mild seasonality around holidays. Overall, Dorothy finds her revenue to be quite dependable and attributes this to the relationships she's built with her customers. The business earns a gross margin of 70% (30% cost), and her monthly overhead is $5,500. That leaves $5,000 profit each month. Quick math ($15,000 x 70% - $5,500 = $5,000).

Included in that overhead are two part-time associates who help run the shop so she can focus on ordering products, maintaining her website, and managing day-to-day operations (bills, payroll, etc.). Dorothy has outsourced bookkeeping duties to an accountant who updates the numbers on a monthly basis, but they don't have too much interaction until tax time.

Click Marketing was founded by Lauren. She is a solo service provider who recently launched her social media marketing company and it is rapidly growing.

Her primary goal is to figure out how to build a team to support her since she sees opportunity for growth but feels constantly overwhelmed by the workload. Lauren knows she's making only a half-hearted attempt to manage the company's finances. Right now, she tracks everything accounting related in Google Sheets, and that is the sum total of her financial management system.

You'll learn more about each of these companies as we parse out each phase of the Process • Plan • Path cycle in greater detail in the coming chapters, and you'll see how each phase can be successfully applied to various types of businesses at different stages and with different goals.

3

PROCESS

I like to start at Process because it encompasses the basic fundamentals of everything. You must define how you operate day to day and examine what inputs and outputs exist in your business in order to have accurate and complete financial statements. Once it's clear that your financial statements are on point, you can be confident that all your decisions are coming from solid, reliable information. And if you're an aspiring entrepreneur, you need to have a firm grasp on your personal finances so you can properly assess the financial risk that lies ahead.

Our main goals in this chapter are to:

- Understand financial statement packages.
- Define an Executive Financial Dashboard.
- Understand who accountants are and what they do.

Though there are numerous components in the Process phase of the accounting cycle, the simplest way to think about it is as the regular financial tasks and reports of your organization that turn transactional data into useful information — a management financial statement package. I want you to know the useful information you need and why you need it, as well as the tasks it takes to complete it so you can better manage your team.

Quality in, quality out.

Before we dive in, though, there's an extremely important concept that you must wrap your mind around: cash basis versus accrual basis accounting.

That may sound like confusing jargon, so I'll break it down.

Cash basis means you are tracking (accounting for) any cash that you receive or spend in your business at the time it is received or spent.

Accrual basis means you are assigning correct time frames to each transaction. For example, an annual insurance premium paid for in one lump sum payment will be put into your monthly log, spreading out that amount over each month — one-twelfth of the total lump sum. (This is also known as the *matching principle*.)

In case this is still a bit confusing, here are a couple examples that might clarify it further:

1. I received my lawyer's monthly bill for $3,500 in September for her time worked in the month of August. I decide to pay the bill in October. *Cash basis* says you have $3,500 of legal expense in October. *Accrual basis* says you have a $3,500 legal expense in August and an accrued expense of $3,500 on your Balance Sheet in August because the payment due is a liability to the company.

2. It's October and I paid my $2,000 monthly rent on the 2nd of the month. Proactively, I paid November rent for the same amount on October 30th. *Cash basis* says you have $4,000 of rent expense in the month of October. *Accrual basis* adjusts the amount to reflect $2,000 in October and $2,000 in November. The $2,000 paid on October 30th is called a *prepaid expense* and is recorded as such on your balance sheet.

As you can see, accrual accounting takes a bit more time and is the most missed opportunity for high-quality accounting. I've noticed that as bookkeeping has become increasingly commoditized, accrual accounting suffers — it's a personal gripe of mine. You get what you pay for, I suppose.

Yes, cash basis accounting is faster and easier to do, but it doesn't paint a clear picture of how the business performed. I know you mostly care about where the money went after it came in and that it was paid on time and everything was in order. But what you'll lack with cash basis accounting are useful metrics from which to measure your business:

- You won't easily determine opportunities to increase profit.
- Monthly and annual financial statements won't be comparable for analysis.
- You won't be able to raise capital or sell your business until you adjust the accounting to accrual basis.

I hope this makes clear why I strongly advocate for accrual basis accounting in your business.

Now that you understand those terms, let's start at the top and work our way down — from the financial statement package to transactional work. And remember: quality in equals quality out. Proper accounting leads to accurate and useful financial statements.

Your financial statement package should comprise five elements:

1. Executive Financial Dashboard (a high-level dashboard of key information)
2. Profit & Loss statement (also referred to as a P&L or Income Statement)
3. Balance sheet
4. Budget with analysis (budget-to-actual and forecast)
5. Supplemental reports you find helpful

Now hang with me in this next part because it may get a bit technical, but I'll simplify the concepts to make it easier to wrap your head around.

I'd like for you to connect each of the components of your financial statement package to specific aspects of your business and to my framework so that each component has a specific purpose, starting with:

Financial Statements

Definition: *Financial statements are the summary of your day-to-day accounting.*

In the beginning, achieving quality financial statements is a constant evolution because we are only as good as the information we have at this particular moment in time. You'll inevitably tweak these reports as they evolve, but the goal as the business owner is to understand *how* you evaluate your business and align the financial statements to a format that makes the most sense to you.

Financial Statements: Profit & Loss

Definition: *At its core, the P&L represents the results of your business model over a certain period of time (a month, a quarter, a year)*

You're probably familiar with the elements that make up a P&L: revenue and expenses, but did you know there are actually four main components it should include?

1. **Revenue:** Earned income generated from your business, which includes discounts and returns.
2. **Cost of sales:** The cost to produce that revenue.
3. **Sales and marketing expenses:** The cost to promote your business, gain new customers, and generate new revenue.
4. **General and administrative expenses (G&A):** The cost of running your business.

Let's look at Slow Drip Coffee as an example for each of these four components.

Their menu includes everything from coffee and espresso drinks, to pastries and prepared food, to apparel. Since these are the three main ways Erin creates income, I advise her to create three sub-categories under the Revenue section of her P&L: Beverages, Food, and Merchandise. These sub-categories represent *how* she makes money, so she doesn't have to be overly detailed in this part of her P&L because that will come in the Supplemental Report part of the financial package.

Another example is my own consulting business's revenue sub-categories that include recurring consulting and project consulting. Why do I separate these? Because I want to easily see the components of how my consulting business is doing. What's my recurring revenue (ongoing) that I can count on versus the project revenue (one-time) that I may or may not be able to depend on in the future?

The single number of *Revenue* as a line item all lumped together doesn't tell a complete story. It's a correct number, but is too high-level and not useful in a practical way.

Cost of sales is what you need to help generate that revenue — think direct materials, direct labor, and the like. For Slow Drip Coffee, Erin's cost of sales numbers include things like the cost of cups, lids, napkins, beans, milk, kitchen supplies, and equipment. Collectively, these are called *direct materials*.

We will also include the barista's pay here (referred to as *direct labor*) because it's an essential part of delivering the final product to the customer. In contrast, a cashier is considered indirect labor and would be classified as General and Administrative. In restaurant terms, it's the difference between your back of house and front of house staff.

IMPORTANT CONCEPT: This cost of sales is the basis from which you will more accurately define your pricing. The value in tracking direct expenses and labor properly is that it shows you the *real* cost of your revenue that you can compare to your *estimate*. So, if your cost of sales is higher than expected — that is, you're paying more to try to make money than the actual money you're bringing in — that's a red flag telling you to look closer at what's going on. For Erin, this may mean that her employees are giving away free coffee, stealing beans, or that she's over-staffed.

Revenue – Cost of Sales = Gross Profit (also known as Net Revenue)

Gross Profit ÷ Revenue = Gross Profit Margin

Each business and industry should establish a target gross profit margin because it is an essential number that helps you budget and measure the results of your business. It tells you how much of each dollar of revenue you get to keep, and it tells you how much you need to make to break even. For this reason, I include a gross profit margin as a component of the Executive Financial Dashboard.

Now, back to Erin.

She dedicated a good chunk of her start-up capital to sales and marketing in an effort to build a customer base. She hired a digital marketing agency at $3,000 per month, printed flyers to hand out at the local farmers market, and bought Facebook ads to promote the new shop.

All of these expenses are logged in the Sales and Marketing section of her P&L. Whenever possible, you want to create mechanisms — such as collecting coupons or using technology within digital ads — to measure the success of and revenue generated from each campaign. This is your Return on Investment (ROI) of the campaign. In other words, was the cost of the marketing campaign worth it? It's important to make this its own section in your Profit & Loss Statement because many of these costs are non-recurring and given a specific purpose in your sales and marketing, and you always want to create the highest-quality records you can.

Finally, there are your General and Administrative Expenses. This includes familiar categories such as auto expenses, rent, insurance, legal and professional fees, travel, and office expenses. Simply put, these are the costs of running your business.

Collectively, Sales & Marketing combined with General and Administrative Expenses are called *Operating Expenses.*

Gross Profit – Operating Expenses = Net Profit

Financial Statements: Balance Sheet
Definition: *The balance sheet is a snapshot of your business at a specific point in time.*

Whereas a P&L covering the period of January 1, 2020–December 31, 2020 represents that entire year, a balance sheet dated December 31, 2020 is specific to that day. And it specifically answers the question, "how is the financial health of my company?" at that point in time.

The balance sheet — and accounting at the highest level — is represented by a simple equation:

Assets = Liabilities + Equity

This is the *balance* part of the balance sheet. Let's define these terms so they're crystal-clear:

- **Asset:** Something that has future value.
- **Liabilities:** Something that has a future cost.
- **Equity:** The net value of the company.

Assets may include cash, accounts receivable, prepaid expenses, inventory, and fixed assets because they are all things that will provide future value. **Cash** is cash, and its value allows you to fund your business operations or make distributions to the owners. **Accounts receivable** are the unpaid invoices for services rendered or product(s) sold, which will also turn into cash. **Prepaid expenses**, like rent paid ahead of time, has the future value of rent. **Inventory** will be sold for cash, and **fixed assets** are significant purchases that have value that extends beyond a year (e.g., a computer, office furniture, a car).

     Liabilities include accounts payable, accrued expenses, credit card balances, loans due to others, and unpaid sales, payroll, and income taxes. These are all things that will require cash in the future. **Accounts payable** are unpaid bills that have not yet come due. **Accrued expenses** are the recording of an expense that has not yet been billed so you can account for it in the period in which it was intended.

     Equity is the value of your company. It's everything you have (assets) minus everything you owe (liabilities). Don't confuse value with *valuation* (which is the market value a buyer would pay for or invest in your business). Our definition of **value** here means that if you were to liquidate all your assets and pay off your liabilities, the net amount of cash left would be the value of your business. The components here would include the accumulated profits from the past, losses, investment taken in, and distributions taken out. And for the math wizards out there: Equity = Assets – Liabilities.

So what does this all mean for you? For one, you don't want to have negative equity because that means you're overleveraged: you have more liabilities than assets — too much debt. Similarly, you may want to keep a certain ratio of assets to liabilities to protect yourself from market fluctuations.

As you learn the various components of your business's finances you'll be better equipped to keep track of what you want to have in each of these balance sheet categories. You'll be able to make necessary adjustments and stabilize the financial wellbeing of your business — and by proximity, your own financial health.

Budgets
Within your monthly financial package, you should pull out the current month's budget from the annual budget and compare it to how the business actually performed during the month — appropriately referred to as *Budget-to-Actual*. Most importantly,

this includes the results of your P&L and major capital expenses and your fixed assets, which are found on your balance sheet.

Ask yourself the following questions:

- Did you hit your revenue goal?
- Did you hit your profit goal?
- Do you have the amount of cash you anticipated?
- Are you on track for year-end financial results?

You want to focus on any differences between your projected budget and the actual results of operations. Then your accountant should prepare an analysis and commentary to explain any significant differences between the two. This is typically the responsibility of a Controller in large organizations.

For example, if legal expenses are more than expected, the commentary might be, "we hired XYZ Law Firm to settle such-and-such lawsuit." I also recommend that you establish a variance threshold that, when you hit it, will trigger you to investigate further. So, if your projected versus actual budget is off by 5 percent *and* $1,000, you'll look deeper. Having the percentage *and* the dollar amount prevents you wasting time on a swing of 30 percent that turns out to be a dollar variance of only $30.

Lastly, when looking at projected versus actual budget variances, consider the impact a big difference will make on your budget for the rest of the year. Will you still hit your target? What areas of the business should you focus on to generate greater profitability, or, in a bad year, to minimize losses?

Supplemental Reports
This one is short and sweet: Supplemental reports are simply the information and data that you can pull from sources inside your company that give you more in-depth details on sales analytics, payroll utilization, the performance of marketing campaigns, and anything else you find to be useful in your organization.

Executive Financial Dashboard
This one-page document is your holy grail. It is a quick look at a handful of pertinent numbers that give you a clear view of the performance and the health of your company every month. It includes a combination of numbers from your P&L and balance sheet, some of which are account balances straight from the financial statement numbers, and some are ratios.

The key numbers you should look at every month include:

- **Cash and cash burn:** How much cash do I have, and when will it run out?
- **Current receivables and payables:** In the short-term, how much money is due to me, and what is due to pay out?

- **Equity:** Graph out the prior 12 months and track the movement (aka, trendline or rolling 12-month).
- **Revenue and margin:** Current month, year to date (YTD), and rolling 12-month (trendline).
- **Operating expenses by category:** Current month, YTD, and rolling 12-month (trendline).
- **Profit:** Current month, YTD, rolling 12-month (trendline), and projected year.

Accounting Cycle

When I talk about the accounting cycle, I am referring to the daily process of recording transactions, making necessary adjustments to have accrual-basis accounting, and creating a financial statement at the end of that cycle summarizing the data.

In accounting language, it breaks down this way:

1. Individual cash-basis transactions aggregate to account balances . . .
2. That are reviewed and adjusted to accrual accounting . . .
3. At which point financial statements are prepared and delivered to you for analysis.

It's worth repeating that quality in equals quality out. This is why everyone has a love-hate relationship with the type-A nature of an accountant.

They want supporting documentation, copies of invoices, contracts, and loan documents to ensure the accuracy and completeness of your data inputs. The thoroughness and document retention may feel tedious at times, but when your accounting team has the insight these details provide, you'll win with a management report that leads to larger profits — something everyone can get behind! Now you're seeing the tangible benefits of putting these elements into place.

Monthly Close Process and Timeline
Like most things in your business, you should have a clear process and timeline around deliverables — in this case, closing your books each month. To do this, of course, you have to know what I mean by "close". For our purposes, it's simply the periodic wrap-up of your accounting, typically completed monthly. Think of this as the checklist of tasks your accountant must complete to ensure quality financial statements, such as:

1. Reconciling bank and credit card accounts so that you know every dollar has been accounted for, and no unauthorized or fraudulent transactions have occurred.
2. Reviewing the details of each financial statement account to ensure that all transactions within are properly recorded in the correct account.

3. Comparing the current month to previous
    months to spot anomalies and variances.
    For example, one month shows an amount for
    rent expense and the following month does
    not. This tells you an accrual is missing
    because rent expense should be the same
    each month.

Not everyone closes their books monthly, but it's one
of the most important things you can do to promptly
respond to unplanned shifts in your financial
position and plan.

It is reasonable to expect this to be completed
two weeks after the end of the month. This provides
time for bank and credit card statements to become
available and for other relevant reports to be
analyzed in a systematic and thorough manner.

Dorothy Rose in the Process Phase

As you'll remember, Dorothy's main goal is to free
up time spent in her business and focus on her vision
of balance in her life. But she has concerns. "How is
the business going to run without me?" she asks.
"I've been behind the counter wearing multiple hats
in the business since the day I opened the doors, and
my customers like to see me here."

I anticipated that Dorothy's biggest challenge
will be transitioning the operations of her business
to her team more than solving the financial

goal because it's the source of her greatest fear — letting go.

The process of letting go, delegating, starts with documenting how things get done before we can do anything around her finances. The more detail she can provide around her processes, the easier it is for her to assign tasks to her team and for them to complete the work properly.

It's essential that she defines a baseline amount of money she'll need from the business on a regular basis for living expenses. No one person's financial situation is the same, so where one person may have inherited a lifetime's sum of money, another person may live paycheck to paycheck, so their monthly financial needs can vary wildly.

Dorothy went through her regular bills and added an amount for travel and fun, finally determining that she needs $5,000 each month to be comfortable. Recall that her business, on average, netted $5,000 profit each month. Factoring in her need to increase the hours worked by her support staff, she's nervous how she will cover the additional payroll and still have enough money left over to pay herself.

So we dive into her business's numbers. I want to make sure the accounting that's been done accurately reflects the profit she anticipates to take. She had never reconciled her books, nor had she carved out all the personal expenses she ran through the business, and it turns out the business was a touch more profitable than she thought — great news!

From there, we built a schedule and determined the additional hours and related cost that would be required to free herself from the business. The result dropped her $5,000 monthly take-home down to $2,000, which caused uneasiness. So we brainstormed. Dorothy thought about missed opportunities she hadn't previously seized due to lack of bandwidth and the simple fact that she was happy with the profit she made.

She recalled customer requests to make weekly deliveries to their offices, which she had initially dismissed since those deliveries would have pulled her away from the shop. But if she was going to reach her new goal of creating balance in her life, she would need to generate more revenue. This led to a deeper conversation around what her business would look like if she had more free time, which helped her sketch out a new business plan that included additional streams of income.

4

PLAN

Be intentional.

You need a plan. You even know some of the things you need a plan for — client deliverables, product mix, a launch schedule, revenue goals, a marketing plan, hiring needs — but maybe you still haven't created one. Maybe it feels overwhelming to consider all the things you need to consider. Maybe you aren't certain what information and which goals to prioritize for where you are in your business's growth. A certain amount of analysis-paralysis sets in and stymies the natural trajectory of your business. This may lead to frustration, prompting you to throw everything at the wall to see what sticks (not a solid strategy, in case you were wondering), or buy multiple online courses that promise to make the way clear. Basically, you try anything to figure out why you aren't where you want to be.

This is all very normal. But also not very productive in the end.

Online courses and business books can lack specificity for your particular business and the particular stage it is in. Just-try-anything approaches are scattershot by definition, and both reveal and create a bit of chaos, which is growth kryptonite. Sure, you can build a business by just starting, but a poor or nonexistent plan might have gaps you don't see.

A more streamlined and tailored planning approach is in order.

The best solution is to think about small milestones that you can realistically achieve. This is true with internal goals for your team, as well as for establishing value (valuation) in your business when raising money.

When I work with clients, we start the planning process by nailing down the core business plan for their type of business (service- or product-based) and expanding from there:

- How do you make money?
- How do you market your business?
- What does it take to run your business (people, software, insurance, etc.)?

If you're not picking up what I'm putting down, I'm talking about a *business plan*. The very term can strike fear into the heart of many entrepreneurs who cringe at the idea of going through this exercise, so let me demystify it for you a bit.

Think of a business plan as a game plan. It's research. It's the foundation from which you communicate who you are and what you do. You can definitely do that, right? Yeah, you can.

If you're a new business, just launching, or in your infancy, you are in a great position to consider something that is now known as a "blue ocean strategy", a phrase coined in the book by the same name. You can also do this if you're further along in the life of your business — you'll just have more moving parts with which to contend, but it's absolutely workable.

A blue ocean strategy means figuring out how your business can home in on a relatively untapped part of your industry that sets you apart from the competition and gives you an edge. The analogy comes from the idea that if most companies are doing the same thing, vying for the same clients — like sharks in the water — that water becomes bloody pretty quickly as they're all circling and attacking each other. (Gross, I know, but it drives home the point really vividly, doesn't it?)

So, you go looking for the blue ocean — the place outside the feeding frenzy where it's clear, open, and free for you to do your thing. A great example of this are the hair salons that only offer blow-outs, that smooth, shiny hairstyle people adore. Most hair salons are full-service: cut, color, style, grooming, but the blow-out salons swam away from this model and focused solely on a very specific — and popular — service. In so doing, they set themselves apart from the others and built a multimillion-dollar industry.

You can see why it's easier at the beginning of your business planning to figure out if there's a way to find your own blue ocean, but there's always room to pivot and grow if you're smart and strategic about it.

And that's what this phase is all about: A clear-eyed look at what you do and how you do it, as well as how you deliver those services to your customers and clients. Do you have a website where they can purchase a service package or product offerings? Who packs and ships physical products? Are there regulation or legal issues you'll need to battle? Who's your competition and what can you learn from them?

I know this seems like a lot of questions, but if you think about it, you can answer most of them off the top of your head. So this phase is really just a way to organize it all into one place, which is actually pretty convenient.

But we're not done yet! Let's also consider your position in the market. Are you a basic commodity or a premium business? A Walmart or a Saks Fifth Avenue?

This obviously influences who you serve and their specific demographics. What are your ideal customers' spending habits around your product or service? What are the psychological drivers that bring them to you, and how can you better address those needs?

After defining your ideal customer, the next logical area to address is pricing. What do you charge for your services or products? The answers to the previous two questions should help inform this to some degree, and so should your revenue goals. Making sure these elements align in your business is going to be a big key to your success. So take the time to do your homework and get this right.

Next, what are your hiring needs to support you achieving these goals, and how much will you pay them? Will you offer bonuses or other incentives?

Finally, how will you market your business? Online? Print ads? Strategic partnerships? And what are the costs attached to each?

Putting in the time now to figure out all these details — while time-consuming — will save you loads of time, energy, money, and frustration in the long run. And this is what I love helping my clients do. Also, it's easier (and, dare I say, more fun?) to have me alongside helping them get clear on each facet of their business.

Lastly, it's important to understand that planning happens on an ongoing basis. Perhaps you're entertaining the idea of expanding a product line or the geographic growth of your organization. All of this should be planned before you act on it in the interest of cash flow and the potential need to raise capital.

Now that you have a more comprehensive view of what to do in the planning phase, let's visit one of the business owners you met earlier to see how their plans evolved.

Slow Drip Coffee

Erin is at an exciting stage with her coffee shop — I love working with entrepreneurs early on! Because she's at the very beginning of her business, I advise her to wait on starting the modeling or budgeting process. At this point, I want her to focus her attention on her business plan before all else. As they say, "But first, coffee."

I ask Erin a bunch of questions that she may or may not have answers to, which are intended to challenge her and find any missing points or oversights. Among other things, I want to understand:

1. Physical space: Is it ready to go? Does it require improvements?
2. Regulation and permits: Do you understand the health permit process, and will that have any effect on the planned opening schedule?
3. Staff and training: Will you need to hire staff? How much time do you need to train them before opening?
4. Hours of operation: Do you have a clear idea how to schedule your staff, including opening and closing?
5. Launch plan: Have you outlined a marketing plan?

These questions allow her to fully consider and plan for all the various aspects of opening her business well. Once she's clear on the answers, we begin to map out the timeline for opening her coffee shop and beyond.

Recall that the framework is a continuous circle and that we always start at the proper point for *your* business. In this case, before the financial path can be determined, the business plan must be concrete. Sure, you may find that some decisions will require a pivot, but you must be clear on the business plan before you begin to budget. This practice helps mitigate unexpected expenses and frustration.

5

PATH

Having your business plan is essential, as you've just learned. But how do you turn that plan into reality? The key is to develop a financial path to get there. Seems pretty obvious, right? But honestly — show of hands — who has actually created a budget and regularly checks in on it? Kudos to you if you have.

If you haven't, that's okay too. You aren't alone. Most companies I've encountered don't either, and if they do, they often never open that spreadsheet again once it's complete. And since cash flow and profits are your most precious commodity, being really strategic about your path *matters*. A lot.

So the first step is to take your strategic plan and factor in everything you intend to execute within your business plan and the milestones you'll achieve along the way.

I'm guessing your next question is *how?*

There are a few tools I use to map out this path, namely financial modeling, budgets, and

Josh Greenbaum

forecasts. That might sound very complex, but really, they're not so scary once you break them down. Let's start with financial modeling.

Financial Modeling
Sometimes people conflate financial modeling with budgeting, and though the difference is small, the distinction is important and helpful to understand.

A financial model highlights a potential section of your business and figures out what it would actually look like as part of your business. So you might ask, "What would it look like if we launched x, y, and z?" This idea can then be isolated and modeled out to understand the financial impact of a new service or product *before* adding it into your entire budget. In this way, you figure out if it will be a smart financial move before you invest (and potentially lose) any money on it.

I did this for my own business. The services included standard accounting and consulting CFO services. I charged a standard rate, and the whole thing was very straightforward.

Then, after more than a year of brainstorming, I had the idea to write this book and expand my services to include group consulting and workshops to address a larger market of small businesses. I wanted to afford small business owners the sophistication of corporate accounting without the typical cost. The research required an understanding of what it takes to write and release a book (I hired a ghostwriter to help), what it takes to build and launch a coaching service (I hired a marketing consultant), and the technology and infrastructure I needed to support it all. Then I had to understand what the revenue side of all this was going to look like. And that was my financial model.

From there, I was able to integrate the new revenue and costs into the existing business model and have a complete budget. Like many small businesses, I then explored financing to fund this growth.

Pro Tip: As you go through the budgeting process, document your assumptions and the thought processes that led you to add something to the list. Then run those by a business partner, a trusted advisor, or your financial consultant to see if those motivations hold up under scrutiny.

Remember, the goal here is to build a business that runs as smartly, efficiently, and *profitably* as possible. The business should also align with the lifestyle you desire. Most of us have at least a couple blind spots or beliefs that interfere with our ability to clearly see our business, goals, or path forward. An outside perspective is invaluable here.

Be sure to anticipate your capital needs along each leg of the path toward reaching your goals and budget them in. Often, the time it takes to raise money is longer than you anticipate. Figure out how you'll manage your cash flow, and factor in any additional expenses related to it.

Once you've nailed this all down, clearly spell out each person's role and responsibilities and then communicate it to them. Making sure all your team members are on the same page is a huge part of your business's ability to reach its goals. Take your time to get this right; check with your team members and clear up any confusion. Also, invite their input as is appropriate, so they feel personally invested in helping you reach your goals.

We touched on budgets a bit while discussing financial modeling, but let's dig in a little more so you fully understand the difference between the two.

Budgets

How often do you ask yourself if it's worth spending the time to create a budget? There are so many assumptions. So many guesses pulled out of thin air, am I right?

Here's the truth of it: There are different kinds of budgets that serve different purposes, and I believe that each budget has a specific value.

To start, **short-term budgets**, also known as *cash flow forecasts*, are defined as those that look at the next three months or less, and their purpose is to focus on cash flow. The objective here is to anticipate the timing of cash coming in and going out, and to manage it closely with your accounting team to make any needed adjustments. I'm a proponent of looking at this as a rolling quarter of the year to use in good times and cash crunches. Each week that passes, you update the prior week with the actual money spent, roll the tracker forward another week, and make adjustments as necessary. In the simplest terms, you plan your cash flow.

Next, an **annual budget** process is really a team sport, projecting for the coming year in every department. Creating one with your team members allows them to participate in your company's financial objectives, get buy-in from them, and create accountability from which to manage.

Here's how I recommend breaking down your annual budget with your team members:

1. The **sales/business development team** forecasts sales, from which your purchasing and resource planning can be made.
2. The **marketing department** outlines their strategy and spending to support the sales goals.
3. The **operations team** projects overall corporate spending and corporate initiatives.

With the head of each group carving out their portion of the budget, you'll get closer to an accurate budget. Your accountant — ideally a CFO — is not the right person to populate your budget. Rather, they will help you manage the budget process, contribute insight, and ask questions to challenge assumptions. And, most importantly, an accurate budget allows you to more closely project your profit. Then, as long as that profit projection aligns with your goals as the owner, you're good to go.

For those of you who have a small organization or the entire team is just you, consult professionals around you in areas for which you're unclear or inexperienced.

I encourage you to map out budgets and combine P&L activity with cash flow. Profits are great, but cash flow is vital. It's also important to bear in mind that for some companies, not all sales result in cash the same day. For retail and restaurants, there's a cash register and money flows in with each sale. Yet service providers and event production, for example, often have delays with payment terms and ticket sales, respectively. Be sure your budget reflects all of these details, including:

- What investment will you take in and when? (Cash in)
- What revenue do you expect to earn, and when will you actually collect it? (Cash in)
- What expenses will you incur and when? (Cash out)
- When are loan payments due (Cash out)

Don't take shortcuts here! Take your time, dig deep, and evaluate every part of your business — be thorough. Trust me: if you do, it will pay literal and figurative dividends because you will be able to use this document as a tool to communicate expectations and timelines to your team.

As part of this process, clearly define and connect each goal to the respective area of the business. This goes beyond simply naming the goal ("hit $1 million in revenue this year") and spells out exactly what you mean by that ("sell 20,000 units" or "raise prices by ten percent"). What will your marketing budget require to achieve that revenue? Will your supply chain support 20,000 units? What's the lead time, and can you get a discount for ordering in bulk?

It's also important to consider your goals for your company and for you personally. Some clients come to me because they need a strategy for exiting their company or reducing their hours without hurting the bottom line. So when I talk about goals, I mean *all* your goals.

Yes, this can feel overwhelming sometimes, and I suspect that's why a lot of people never do it: analysis paralysis. We've all been there at one time or another — I've done it myself! — but having a clear roadmap to follow and someone to go through the process with you makes it much more manageable.

Trust me, you CAN do this!

Forecasting
Finally, forecasts, or long-term budgets, project out the next three to five years and communicate the strategy and direction a business aims to go. The

assumptions here may feel baseless and usually reflect executive-level thought leadership, markets, the economy, and future opportunities. You may evaluate if a line of business has become less relevant now and needs to phase out, or if some technological innovation will allow you to augment and streamline your operations. Take your time to consider all the relevant factors when laying out your long-term budget.

There's potentially a lot of information that goes into your various budgets, so having someone walk you through one will likely show you that it's far more manageable than you might have previously thought. As I keep mentioning, I strongly encourage you to bring in others to contribute their experience and knowledge base and identify the smartest ways to get to those important markers and milestones.

Now let's look at some criteria Lauren had to decide on as she moved into the financial path stage.

Click Marketing

When embarking on growth in a small business — and in this case, a service-based one run entirely by a single person — it's best to first look at core competencies, deliverables, and how revenue is derived.

Lauren had a solid business plan and was ready to grow. So, in terms of our framework, it was time for her to move from Plan to Path. We needed to model out her growth and map her costs and cash flow so she wouldn't overextend herself and bleed her bank account dry.

We looked at core competencies first because this helped her home in on what she's good and bad at, and further, what responsibilities within the day-to-day business she enjoyed, and those she despised. As business owners, I know we all love to hold tight to every little thing, but that approach is what's draining you! Let me be more specific: when scaling, there are different directions Lauren could go:

1. She could hire an assistant to take administrative work off her plate.
2. In this case, she could hire a junior marketing professional to handle client work.
3. She could hire a peer to generate income and deliver client work.
4. She could bring on a partner in exchange for ownership or profit sharing.

I believe the best way to determine the right role is to examine the last two elements: deliverables and how the company derives revenue. From a purely financial perspective, who will have a greater impact on the bottom line?

1. If Lauren feels buried by non-revenue–generating tasks, I'd suggest an assistant.
2. When the client work is constant and the deliverables are easy to delegate, repeatable,

or templated, a junior marketing professional will free up time to find more clients.

3.   Perhaps there's not much to do outside of client work, and since Lauren has built great systems, I'd recommend finding a peer (or acquiring a similar business) and folding them into her processes.

4.   A partner may make sense when it's time to expand into a new market (geographically or in the industry served).

Each case has different financial implications, so the model differs depending on which way she'll go. As I always remind my clients, keep your personal goals in mind when you develop business goals, because more people present more to manage. Keep it all aligned.

PART II

_____

Action Plan

6

WHERE TO START

Now that we've gone through the big-picture concepts and detailed explanations, I want to give you a roadmap that outlines how to begin implementing these best practices.

1. Take stock of where you are today: money in, money out, and your people.
2. Define short- and long-term goals so you know where you're headed.
3. Ensure your processes are good and that you're working with quality numbers.
4. Establish milestones and a timeline.
5. Create your financial path to achieve the goals you've laid out.

When I begin with a new client, I find it most important to meet them where they are and take stock of their overall business. No matter how messy and inefficient processes may seem, something about it works for them, and I never want to rock the boat of day-to-day operations at first.

We talk through the key elements around how money moves: revenue, expenses, and team members. My objective here is to understand the parties and documents involved, the frequency of transactions, and internal process and approval flow. It's important that the appropriate people have eyes on relevant areas. This may often be you if the team is smaller.

In many cases, I would suggest you document how you run your business, step-by-step, both so you can easily delegate tasks in the future and protect yourself in case someone is hit by the proverbial bus. It sounds tragic, but if a key member of your team processes payments and no one else knows how, you'll be frantic to re-create the process if they suddenly can't.

From there, we talk about the overall goals and objectives. These may be as simple as, "I just want to see a P&L" to "I want to grow my profit by $100,000". These are all good goals, and now we now have a target from which to work backward.

At this point we dive into the Process phase to ensure we have good numbers, then we move forward with a Plan.

- Make sure your bank and credit card accounts are reconciled so we know all your transactions are in. (Completeness)
- Review your P&L and balance sheet accounts to ensure the detailed transactions within are classified correctly. (Accuracy)
- Take into consideration what may be missing.

Because you're each in a different place in your business, I can't speak to the infinite scenarios you want to accomplish. Rather, I hope you find that my framework gives you a clear starting point and a road map ahead.

7

FINANCING YOUR BUSINESS

I bet you have many questions about financing. It's a
scary area for people to discuss debt and equity, so
let me give you some guidelines that will provide
perspective. The reason people raise outside money
is that it provides an endless list of opportunities,
including:

- Startup capital to launch your business.
- Additional rounds of funding to grow your
  business.
- Advancing cash on future receivables (known
  as factoring).
- Inventory purchase.
- Building a new website.
- Acquiring a business.

There are three ways to finance a company:

1. Self-funded
2. Debt
3. Equity

Self-funded financing should be fairly self-explanatory: You take your own cash and put it into the business. This feels the scariest because the risk falls squarely on your shoulders. On the flip side, you own one hundred percent of your company.

Debt financing includes credit cards, lines of credit, and general loans. Each of these will typically require a personal guarantee by a bank, which means that if things go sideways with the business, you're still on the hook personally. This is less risky than self-funding because you're using the bank's cash and keeping your money in your pocket, but for this reduced risk, you'll pay interest. However, you still own one-hundred percent of your company.

Equity financing brings investors into the mix. Investors have a higher risk threshold than a bank and may fund a business when banks will not. This option, like debt financing, spreads the risk to someone other than yourself. Different from the two previous examples, however, you'll give up a percentage of your company to an investor.

So how should you consider these options? How do you decide the best route? There's no quick and simple answer, but there are some general truths on which you can rely. Debt financing will typically result in a monthly payment, so you'll need to factor that into your cash flow tracker to make sure you can afford it. And when you identify the right equity investor, that person should bring in more than money, they should add value that will drive additional growth and profit.

The other truth to consider is your return on investment (ROI). Any financing activity (investment) must result in a positive return, otherwise you're losing money. Let's play this out in a scenario.

Assume you need $500,000 to build a new website, hire a sales team, and create marketing material for a new line of service to your existing business. The business has $1,000,000 in the bank. Recall our three options for financing: self, debt, and equity.

Self-funding may feel too risky because you've just earmarked half your cash for a new venture. So the best routes are probably debt or equity. Current loan rates estimate a ten-percent annual interest rate for a ten-year loan. Also, you hired a valuation specialist and learned your business is valued at $1,500,000. If you bring in an investor, you might have to give that person one-third of your entire business — forever — and you'll have no direct payback on that investment. If your new line of business will return sufficient cash flow to support the monthly payment of a loan, it may be a better return compared to your loss of equity.

It's important to know that investment capital doesn't always mean launch and growth in the conventional sense; it also refers to how you allocate money (capital). Should you self-invest in a team of people? Will that team allow you to generate exponential profit? Is the greater profit a better return on your current situation?

As a separate example, think about inventory for a moment. Your company manufactures watches in China that you retail direct-to-consumer through your website. They offer you a large discount for a bulk order, which will consume a large amount of your cash. Should you make that investment? Again, not a quick and simple answer because you need to think about cash flow: you're sinking today's cash into inventory, and inventory is an asset, which means it has future value. So you have to think about how soon you will turn that inventory into revenue (cash and profit).

Really take time to think through these things. Try not to let it overwhelm you, but consider it from a practical perspective. Why start something with a poor ROI? Why continue something with a poor ROI?

This is why you will model ideas out and not rely on gut feelings.

This is why you must set up your accounting system in a way that tells the *real* story of your business.

This is why you want to maintain your books on an accrual basis and review them on a monthly basis.

And this is why you need a management report with key performance indicators.

8

MAINTENANCE AND MOVING FORWARD

Financial leadership is found in the maintenance
and management of accounting processes. You can
create the most perfect processes from the get-go,
but unless you periodically check in, you won't
necessarily achieve your goals.

Maintenance comes in monthly financial
meetings where you zoom in, and quarterly strategy
sessions where you zoom out. You zoom in to
understand the results of the prior month (looking
backward), comparing results to your budget, and
making necessary adjustments to stay the course.
You zoom out to consider your industry, the
economy, the direction of the market, and strategic
planning for the future (looking ahead).

Monthly financial meetings are preceded
with a monthly close checklist. I spoke about this
in the Process section and, to reiterate, it's your

accountant's list of things to do to ensure you have complete and accurate financial statements.

Why should you care about this list? Because it's how you will manage your team; it's good financial leadership. Teams perform better when they know they're being monitored. Quite frankly, a review of that close list may even be a good starting point in your financial meeting to give everyone a chance to ask questions about anomalies and questionable transactions.

The closing checklist includes, but is not limited to:

- Reconciling cash and credit card accounts.
- Reviewing outstanding money owed to the company.
- Taking an inventory count.
- Recording accruals (remember, accrual accounting optimizes the books using the matching principle).
- Reviewing each account on the P&L to ensure transactions were recorded in the appropriate account.
- Comparing the actual results of the month to the budget and explaining any variances.
- Preparing supplemental schedules as requested by management.
- Calculating key performance indicators for the Executive Financial Dashboard.

We also talked about the strategic nature of quarterly meetings earlier. Throughout the year, prioritize time to plan. Give yourself space from the day-to-day business and look at the big picture. Set goals and write them down. We all know how easy it is to get lost in the daily grind and watch time fly, so be intentional about this.

I think of each quarter as having a specific objective. Summer is for dreaming big, strategizing, and looking at the picture as a whole. Fall is for budgeting, taking those notes from summertime and turning them into an action plan. Winter brings the wrap-up of the year and tax preparation before the end of December. Spring is a time to check in and see how your milestones and timelines are progressing.

CONCLUSION

I wholeheartedly appreciate the time you took
to read this book. I hope you found it valuable,
informative, and approachable. Business and
personal finance is often a taboo subject for people
filled with deep-rooted issues of shame and
embarrassment. But it's so worth it to work through
those feelings and look past mistakes. They
happened for a reason and brought you to today
where you have the opportunity to effect the change
you deserve.

You've taken the first step to radically
improving your financial position in the world, and
now that you have a clearer understanding of what
all those accounting terms mean and how they work
on a practical level in your business, you no longer
have to let the fear of money or numbers affect you
in the future.

You are fully capable of taking charge and being an impactful force in the market.

And I want you to know that I am here to support you all the way to the top — to mentor, guide, and challenge you to be the best version of yourself every single day.

You *will* have the life you imagined, with all the money and success that previously felt unreachable, with a little intention and purpose.

Because you are now CFO Minded.

GENERAL TERMS AND CONCEPTS

Here's a list of terms, concepts, and KPIs that you should put into practice. Like everything, there's much more you can add to the list, but this will get you started.

Financial Statements and Other Related Reports & Terms

Methodology
- Cash-basis accounting: Cash accounting is a method that records transactions only in the period when cash is received or paid.
- Accrual-basis accounting: Accrual accounting is a method of accounting that records transactions and other events and circumstances in the periods in which they

occur, rather than the one-time period in which cash is received or paid.

Balance Sheet
- Accounting equation: Assets = Liabilities + Equity

Assets
- Assets: A resource that provides current or future economic value.
- Current assets: Cash and other assets that are expected to be converted to cash or provide value within a year.
- Accounts receivable: Money owed to a company by a customer (typically an unpaid invoice).
- Prepaid expenses: Money paid for future services to be rendered within a year.
- Inventory: Raw materials and goods available for sale recorded at acquisition cost or cost to produce.
- Investments: Represents the company's investment in private or public ownership of stocks, bonds, and real estate with the intent of receiving back the purchase price plus an increase in the form of dividends, interest, or gains from appreciation upon sale or maturity.
- Fixed assets: Tangible items which are purchased for long-term use in the operations

of a business. Examples are furniture, buildings, cars, machinery, and equipment. These are depreciated (expensed) over

- the item's useful life, which is greater than one year.
- Intangible assets: An asset that is not physical in nature, such as goodwill, brand recognition, and intellectual property, including patents, trademarks, and copyrights. These are amortized, expensed, over fifteen years.
- Depreciation (accumulated depreciation): A systematic reduction in the value of an asset with the passage of time. For example, a new computer with a three-year life is depreciated (expensed) at 1/36th of the original cost each month. Accumulated depreciation is the total amount of monthly depreciation.
- Other assets: Assets that cannot be classified as current assets, fixed assets, or intangible assets with an economic value exceeding one year. Example: A security deposit on a five-year office lease.

Liabilities
- Accounts payable: Bills not yet paid; amount owed to a creditor from buying goods and services in the normal course of business.
- Accrued expenses: The process to account for an expense that has not yet been billed by a

vendor. The expense is recorded (accrued) in the accounting period in which it occurred.

- Sales tax payable: A liability in the balance sheet that keeps track of the sales tax collected from customers and is held for remittance to the government on a timely basis. Sales tax charged to customers is not revenue.
- Credit card: Money a company owes for purchases made by credit card.
- Line of credit: Bank loan that is a short-term, flexible loan that a business can use, as needed, to borrow up to a preset amount of money.
- Loan: A sum of cash borrowed from a bank or lender that is paid back over a term with a stated interest rate.

Equity

- Contributed capital: Cash and other assets that shareholders have given a company in exchange for stock. This is the price that shareholders paid for their stake in the company.
- Distributions: A portion of the profits a company decides to give to its shareholders or a business owners' withdrawal of profits for personal use.
- Retained earning: The portion of profits that a company chooses to keep in the business.

Profit & Loss
- Revenue: Total amount of income generated by the sale of goods or services related to the company's primary operations
- Cost of sales (cost of goods sold): Cost to directly produce revenue not involved in the operations of a business. Cost of a product to a distributor, manufacturer, or retailer. This is where inventory on the balance sheet is expensed once sold. Also referred to as *direct material* and *direct labor* or *prime costs*.
- Gross profit: Profit a company makes after deducting the costs associated with making and selling its products, or the costs associated with providing its services.
- Operating expenses: Expenses a business incurs through its normal operations. Often abbreviated as OpEx, this includes sales and marketing, as well as general and administrative expenses.
- Sales and marketing expenses: Expenses that are the direct result of efforts to grow revenue and expand business development.
- General and administrative expenses: Expenses that are incurred to operate a business.
- Net profit: The actual profit after deducting cost of sales and operating expenses from revenue.

Other Related Reports & Terms

- Accounting receivable aging (AR aging): A report of all outstanding money owed by customers to a company organized in time blocks. For example: Current, 30, 45, 60, 90, and more than 90 days past due.
- Allowance for doubtful accounts: The percentage probability of collection based on past collection history and management judgment. There may be a 90% likelihood that an account 30 days past due will be collected, while the probability drops to 25% when the account is over 90 days past due. Therefore, an assumption that 10% of total receivables 30 days past due are uncollectible establishes a realistic expectation of the asset's value.
- Accounts payable aging (AP aging): A report of all outstanding money owed to vendors organized in time blocks. For example: Current, 30, 45, 60, 90, and more than 90 days past due.

Budget & Forecasts

- Cash flow tracker: The process to forecast anticipated income and expenses on a cash basis to project potential cash deficits.
- Annual budget: A plan laid out for a company's income and expenses for a financial year.

- Budget-to-actual: The process of comparing results of operations over a specific period to anticipated results through budgets.
- Financial model: The task of building an abstract representation of a real-world financial situation for the purpose of understanding financial opportunity and impact. Typically applied to a segment of the business.
- Forecast: A plan laid out for a company's income and expenses into the future. Typically over a three- to five-year period.

Ratios & Metrics

Operations & Performance
- Gross profit margin: Metric analysis used to assess a company's financial health. Calculated by taking gross profit divided by revenue.
- Contribution margin: A product's price minus all associated variable costs, resulting in the incremental profit earned for each unit sold. Similar to gross profit margin, but related to a specific product, service, or line of business.
- Net profit margin: Ratio of net profits to revenues for a company. Calculated by dividing the net profits by net sales.
- Product (service) mix: An understanding or analysis of revenue based on various

products or services sold. To be examined alongside contribution margin.

- Return on investment (ROI): A profitability ratio that measures the productivity of assets in producing income and the efficiency of use of invested capital. However, it is most commonly used to measure the performance of investment centers. This is calculated by dividing the profit earned on an investment by the cost of that investment.
- Working capital: The measurement, expressed as a dollar amount, to determine money available to meet your current short-term obligations. Calculation: Current assets – current liabilities.
- Quick ratio: The measurement, expressed as a percentage, to determine immediate liquidity. Calculation: Cash + accounts receivable / current liabilities

Cash Flow
- Cash burn: Rate at which a company is spending money. This is typically expressed in monthly terms.
- Days sales outstanding (DSO): A measure that indicates the average number of days that it takes a company to collect payment after a sale has been made. Calculation: Average accounts receivable / revenue x number of days in accounting period.

- Days payables outstanding (DPO): A measure that indicates the average number of days that a company takes to pay its bills. Calculation: Average accounts payable/ cost of goods sold x number of days in accounting period.

ACKNOWLEDGEMENTS

Thank you for taking time to read this. It's
my mission to bring financial leadership to
small business owners because they are the ones who
make the world go round. Business owners like you
are the pulse of your communities and the spirit of
innovation. Specifically those folks who allow me to
stand by their side through the journey we call
business, your ambition and creativity is inspiring.

In writing this book, I was reminded to
forever be bold. It was quite an undertaking to
envision the goal of this book and to translate those
thoughts into words. Handing over earlier drafts to
trusted friends and colleagues was a huge moment of
vulnerability, but I was certain doing so would
improve the finish product — and it did! I'm
constantly grateful to have a supportive network of
people who are always at my side.

Like many things in life, we're only as good as those with whom we surround ourselves, and I had the dream team. Thank you most of all to Meredith Watkins, my collaborative writer and editor. She organized my thoughts, challenged me to simplify complex ideas to make this book a useful tool for all business owners and aspiring entrepreneurs, and brought together the consultants and resources I needed to succeed!

Made in the USA
Middletown, DE
17 January 2022

58903239R00060